A CHILDREN'S CATECHESIS
YEAR ONE—BIBLICAL HISTORY

A GUIDE FOR KIDS AND PARENTS

Karina Ingrid Taylor

GLOSSAHOUSE
WILMORE, KY
www.glossahouse.com

A Children's Catechesis Year One—Biblical History: A Guide for Kids and Parents

GlossaHouse, LLC
110 Callis Circle
Wilmore, KY 40390

Publisher's Cataloging-in-Publication Data
Taylor, Karina Ingrid.
A Children's Catechesis Year One—Biblical History: A Guide for Kids and Parents / Karina Ingrid Taylor, Wilmore, KY: GlossaHouse, ©2023

viii, 50 pages ; 22 cm.– (SERIES)

ISBN: 978-1-63663-055-7 (paperback)

1. Bible. Catechism. I. Title. II. Series.

Library of Congress Control Number:

Cover Design by T. Michael W. Halcomb

Book Layout and volume editing by Fredrick J. Long

*Parents, remember you are your child's greatest teacher
and aside from God, you know them the best.*

*To all the parents and children who will be learning from this Catechesis,
I hope you wonder with them, research with them,
love discovering with them and ask questions!*

May you enjoy using this as much as I enjoyed creating it!

**The Lord bless you and keep you;
the Lord make his face to shine upon you and be gracious to you;
the Lord lift up his countenance upon you and give you peace.**

Numbers 6:24–26

Acknowledgements

I would like to acknowledge Caleb Taylor, my husband, you have always been an encouragement to me. He believes I can do anything. Thank you for your editing and academic support. I came up with this curriculum idea a few years ago through the inspiration of our homeschool curriculum and without discernment from God and my husband's support, I would not have pushed forward to complete it. Thank you to my girls, my family, and my friends for cheering me on. Thank you to our friend, Dr. Fredrick Long, for his academic support, editing, publishing, and our time chatting about biblical history. Thank you to Dr. Lawson Stone for your academic support and edits. A thank you is due to my Rector, Rev. Rick Durrance, for taking the time to pray for me and listen and talk about my ideas.

Table of Contents

Introduction

Dear parents, godparents, and church family,

This guide will be used in Sunday school, but most importantly, it will become a handy tool to use at home every week within the family unit. With the church's support, the information in this guide is to help your kids along in the Christian faith through classical catechetical instruction. Centuries ago, catechesis was the norm for both adults and children, and it is still just as effective. Kids love to recite and memorize; these are the formative years for them to build this strong foundation that will lead to better understanding later.

The catechesis information has been taken from both the 1662 Book of Common Prayer and *To be a Christian: An Anglican Catechism*. For the Baptism section, the English wording has been updated. Informational sentences summarize the biblical story from Scripture to help your kids put in perspective the timeline of events. Many of these sentences have scripture references for additional reading and deeper discussion. This guide takes you through a 40-week curriculum. Each week's information will be introduced on Sunday and is encouraged to be reviewed at home during the week.

Explanation of the Layout and its Use

Through the week you are encouraged to work at home alongside your child. Set a timer for 20 minutes! There are many different techniques to use at home that will aid in memorization, perfection is not key but simply repetition. Start with 4 mins of review time for each section; the bible verse, catechesis, and biblical history with the goal to repeat each section 7 times. Don't forget to review the previous weeks' information, at least three weeks back if possible. Use the note section at the bottom to jot down what memorization methods worked well for you, additional scripture that you found, or praise moments.

Tips for memorization:

1. For active kids, using exercises while reciting can be very helpful (jumping jacks, high-knees, arm circles, marching in place).
2. Have fun making up some hand motions.
3. Writing on a whiteboard and erasing a few words at a time as you keep repeating to help with retention.
4. Singing the recitation to your own tune or a piece of music.
5. Have your kids suggest some silly voices to use while reciting the information.

To see such ideas in action, visit this YouTube channel: Karina Taylor @karinataylor3092

BAPTISM

(Weeks 1–2)

WEEK 1

Bible Verse

For the LORD gives wisdom;

from his mouth comes knowledge and understanding.

Proverbs 2:6

Catechesis

What did your church do for you?

They promised three things in my name.

1. First, that I should renounce the devil and all his works;

2. Second, I should trust God wholeheartedly; and

3. Third, I should serve him faithfully.

The church, my parents, and my godparents will help me understand the meaning of these vows and of the Faith. They promise to help me put my faith in Jesus Christ, and learn the Creeds, the Lord's Prayer, the Ten Commandments, and all other things that a Christian ought to know, believe, and do for the welfare of my soul.

Biblical History

Tell me about God and creation.

Before us and everything, there was God, Jesus, and the Holy Spirit together in love. God created light, Heaven, Earth and plants, the universe, fish and birds, animals, and people, and on the seventh day, he rested. (Genesis 1)

NOTES:

WEEK 2

Bible Verse

For the LORD gives wisdom;

from his mouth comes knowledge and understanding.

Proverbs 2:6

Catechesis

Do you think that you are bound to believe and do as your church, parents, and godparents promised you?

Yes, and with God's help, I will. And I thank our Heavenly Father, who called me to my salvation through Jesus Christ our Savior, and I pray that God will give me his grace that I might continue until he calls me home.

Biblical History

Tell me about creation and the Garden of Eden.

Here on Earth, God formed man from dust and planted a garden called Eden. In this garden, he rooted the tree of life and the tree of knowledge of good and evil. In the Garden of Eden, the man was told by God to work and keep it. The Lord God commanded him to eat fruit from every tree except the Tree of the Knowledge of Good and Evil, or he would die. God did not want him to be alone, so he created a woman from the man's rib. (Genesis 2)

NOTES:

Apostles' Creed

(Weeks 3–12)

WEEK 3

Apostles' Creed

<table>
<tr><td>

I believe in God, the Father almighty,
creator of heaven and earth.
I believe in Jesus Christ, his only Son, our Lord.
He was conceived by the Holy Spirit
and born of the Virgin Mary.
He suffered under Pontius Pilate,
was crucified, died, and was buried.
He descended to the dead.
On the third day, he rose again.
He ascended into heaven,
and is seated at the right hand of the Father.
He will come again to judge the living and the dead.
I believe in the Holy Spirit,
the holy catholic Church,
the communion of saints,
the forgiveness of sins,
the resurrection of the body,
and the life everlasting. Amen.

</td><td>

Father

Son

Holy Spirit

</td></tr>
</table>

Catechesis

What do you chiefly learn in the Articles of Belief?

First, I learn to believe in God the Father, who made me and all the world.
Secondly, in God the Son who redeemed me and all humankind.
Thirdly, in God, the Holy Spirit, who sanctifies me and all God's people.

Biblical History

Tell me about the Fall and Cain and Abel.

In the Garden of Eden, the serpent convinced the woman and man to eat the fruit from the Tree of the Knowledge of Good and Evil. After disobeying God, the Lord cursed the serpent, the man, and the woman and sent them out of the Garden of Eden. The man, Adam, called his wife Eve, and they had two sons, Cain and Abel. Both brothers made sacrifices to God, but Abel's was favored. Because of jealousy, Cain murdered Abel and was then punished to wander for his whole life. (Genesis 3–4)

WEEK 4

Apostles' Creed

<table>
<tr><td>

I believe in God, the Father almighty,
creator of heaven and earth.
I believe in Jesus Christ, his only Son, our Lord.
He was conceived by the Holy Spirit
and born of the Virgin Mary.
He suffered under Pontius Pilate,
was crucified, died, and was buried.
He descended to the dead.
On the third day, he rose again.
He ascended into heaven,
and is seated at the right hand of the Father.
He will come again to judge the living and the dead.
I believe in the Holy Spirit,
the holy catholic Church,
the communion of saints,
the forgiveness of sins,
the resurrection of the body,
and the life everlasting. Amen.

</td><td>

Father

Son

Holy Spirit

</td></tr>
</table>

Catechesis

Who is God?

God is one divine Being eternally existing in three divine Persons: the Father, the Son, and the Holy Spirit. This is the Holy Trinity. (#38) (Matthew 3:16–17; 28:19)

Biblical History

Tell me about Noah and the Flood.

God's people became corrupt and violent, so he decided to send a flood as punishment. But a righteous man named Noah and his family were spared by God. Noah was commanded by God to build an ark and fill it with two of every kind of animal. God sent rain for forty days and forty nights, and when the waters subsided, Noah's ark rested on the top of a mountain. Then the Lord sent a rainbow as a sign that he will never send a flood that destroys all life again. (Genesis 6–10)

WEEK 5

Apostles' Creed

I believe in God, the Father almighty, creator of heaven and earth. **I believe in Jesus Christ, his only Son, our Lord.** He was conceived by the Holy Spirit and born of the Virgin Mary. He suffered under Pontius Pilate, was crucified, died, and was buried. He descended to the dead. On the third day, he rose again. He ascended into heaven, and is seated at the right hand of the Father. He will come again to judge the living and the dead. **I believe in the Holy Spirit,** the holy catholic Church, the communion of saints, the forgiveness of sins, the resurrection of the body, and the life everlasting. Amen.	**Father** **Son** **Holy Spirit**

Catechesis

Who is Jesus Christ?

Jesus Christ is the eternal Word and Son of God, the second Person of the Holy Trinity. He took on human flesh to be the Savior and Redeemer of the world, the only Mediator between God and fallen mankind. (#49) (John 1:14; 14:6; 1 Peter 1:18–19; 1 Timothy 2:5)

Biblical History

Tell me about the Tower of Babel.

In the ancient kingdom of Sumer, Noah's descendants decided to build a tower to reach heaven. The people wanted to make a name for themselves rather than honoring God. Seeing this, God was unhappy. He confused their language so they could no longer understand each other and scattered them over the earth. (Genesis 11)

WEEK 6

Apostles' Creed

<table>
<tr><td>

I believe in God, the Father almighty,
creator of heaven and earth.
I believe in Jesus Christ, his only Son, our Lord.
He was conceived by the Holy Spirit
and born of the Virgin Mary.
He suffered under Pontius Pilate,
was crucified, died, and was buried.
He descended to the dead.
On the third day, he rose again.
He ascended into heaven,
and is seated at the right hand of the Father.
He will come again to judge the living and the dead.
I believe in the Holy Spirit,
the holy catholic Church,
the communion of saints,
the forgiveness of sins,
the resurrection of the body,
and the life everlasting. Amen.

</td><td>

Father

Son

Holy Spirit

</td></tr>
</table>

Catechesis

How was Jesus conceived by the Holy Spirit?

Through the creative power of the Holy Spirit, the eternal Son assumed a fully human nature from his mother, Mary, in personal union with his fully divine nature at the moment of conception in Mary's womb. Jesus is both fully God and fully human. (#54) (Luke 1:34–35)

Biblical History

Tell me about the Patriarchs of Israel.

The history of the patriarchal age was focused on the lives of Abraham, Isaac, and Jacob. God made a covenant with Abram, who was later named Abraham. God promised to give Abram land, a big family, and that his family would become a blessing to the world. Abraham, his son Isaac, and his grandson Jacob were the founders of the people of Israel.

WEEK 7

Apostles' Creed

I believe in God, the Father almighty, creator of heaven and earth. **I believe in Jesus Christ, his only Son, our Lord.** He was conceived by the Holy Spirit and born of the Virgin Mary. He suffered under Pontius Pilate, was crucified, died, and was buried. He descended to the dead. On the third day, he rose again. He ascended into heaven, and is seated at the right hand of the Father. He will come again to judge the living and the dead. **I believe in the Holy Spirit,** the holy catholic Church, the communion of saints, the forgiveness of sins, the resurrection of the body, and the life everlasting. Amen.	**Father** **Son** **Holy Spirit**

Catechesis

Why did Jesus suffer?

Jesus suffered for our sins so that we could have peace with God, as prophesied in the Old Testament. (#57) (Isaiah 53:5)

Biblical History

Tell me about the call of Abraham.

God called Abraham to do many things. God made a covenant with Abram. God promised Abram that his family would become a great nation, and Abram promised to have faith in God and leave his home. After many tests, God renamed Abram to Abraham, and told him to take his only son, Isaac, to be sacrificed. Because Abraham feared God, he obeyed, and God called down from heaven and sent him a ram to sacrifice instead.

WEEK 8

Apostles' Creed

<table>
<tr><td>

I believe in God, the Father almighty,
creator of heaven and earth.
I believe in Jesus Christ, his only Son, our Lord.
He was conceived by the Holy Spirit
and born of the Virgin Mary.
He suffered under Pontius Pilate,
was crucified, died, and was buried.
He descended to the dead.
On the third day, he rose again.
He ascended into heaven,
and is seated at the right hand of the Father.
He will come again to judge the living and the dead.
I believe in the Holy Spirit,
the holy catholic Church,
the communion of saints,
the forgiveness of sins,
the resurrection of the body,
and the life everlasting. Amen.

</td><td>

Father

Son

Holy Spirit

</td></tr>
</table>

Catechesis

What does the Creed mean when it affirms that Jesus rose again from the dead?

It means that Jesus was not simply resuscitated; God restored him physically from death to life in his perfected and glorious body, never to die again. His tomb was empty; Jesus had risen bodily from the dead. The risen Jesus was seen by his apostles and hundreds of other witnesses. (#64) (1 Corinthians 15:3–8)

Biblical History

Tell me about Moses and the Burning Bush.

While shepherding sheep, Moses found a bush that was on fire but did not burn up. God's voice called to Moses from the bush and explained to him that he must go to Egypt to deliver the Israelites from slavery and lead them to the Promised Land of Canaan. (Exodus 2–6)

WEEK 9

Apostles' Creed

I believe in God, the Father almighty, creator of heaven and earth. **I believe in Jesus Christ, his only Son, our Lord.** He was conceived by the Holy Spirit and born of the Virgin Mary. He suffered under Pontius Pilate, was crucified, died, and was buried. He descended to the dead. On the third day, he rose again. He ascended into heaven, and is seated at the right hand of the Father. He will come again to judge the living and the dead. **I believe in the Holy Spirit,** the holy catholic Church, the communion of saints, the forgiveness of sins, the resurrection of the body, and the life everlasting. Amen.	**Father** **Son** **Holy Spirit**

Catechesis

What is the result of the Ascension?

Jesus ascended into heaven so that, through him, his Father might send us the gift of the Holy Spirit. Through the Holy Spirit, Christians are united as Christ's Body on earth to Jesus, our ascended and living High Priest, and to one another. (#67) (1 Corinthians 12:12–13, 27; Ephesians 4:15–16; John 14:15–29; 15:5–9)

Biblical History

Tell me about Pharaoh and the Ten Plagues.

Moses asked Pharaoh to free the Israelites from slavery, but Pharoah refused. God sent ten plagues to Egypt, starting with the Nile River turning to blood, then frogs, gnats, flies, the livestock got sick and died, boils, a hailstorm, locusts, three days of darkness, and finally the death of every firstborn son. The Israelites were instructed to prepare for the Exodus and paint lamb's blood on their doorposts so the angel of death would pass over their home. (Exodus 3:10–15:21)

WEEK 10

Apostles' Creed

I believe in God, the Father almighty, creator of heaven and earth. **I believe in Jesus Christ, his only Son, our Lord.** He was conceived by the Holy Spirit and born of the Virgin Mary. He suffered under Pontius Pilate, was crucified, died, and was buried. He descended to the dead. On the third day, he rose again. He ascended into heaven, and is seated at the right hand of the Father. He will come again to judge the living and the dead. **I believe in the Holy Spirit,** the holy catholic Church, the communion of saints, the forgiveness of sins, the resurrection of the body, and the life everlasting. Amen.	**Father** **Son** **Holy Spirit**

Catechesis

Who is the Holy Spirit?

God the Holy Spirit is the third Person in the Holy Trinity, co-equal and co-eternal with God the Father and God the Son, and equally worthy of our honor and worship. (#81) (Luke 11:13; John 14:26; 16:7)

Biblical History

Tell me about Exodus and the Song of Moses and Miriam.

Moses led the Israelites out of Egypt to freedom, providing safe passage through the Red Sea with God's help. This was the day the Lord saved Israel, the day the Israelites feared the Lord, and the day they put their trust in him. After they were saved, Moses and his sister Miriam led the Israelites to sing a song praising God's faithfulness. (Exodus 15:1–21)

WEEK 11

Apostles' Creed

<table>
<tr><td>

I believe in God, the Father almighty,
creator of heaven and earth.
I believe in Jesus Christ, his only Son, our Lord.
He was conceived by the Holy Spirit
and born of the Virgin Mary.
He suffered under Pontius Pilate,
was crucified, died, and was buried.
He descended to the dead.
On the third day, he rose again.
He ascended into heaven,
and is seated at the right hand of the Father.
He will come again to judge the living and the dead.
I believe in the Holy Spirit,
the holy catholic Church,
the communion of saints,
the forgiveness of sins,
the resurrection of the body,
and the life everlasting. Amen.

</td><td>

Father

Son

Holy Spirit

</td></tr>
</table>

Catechesis

Why is the Church called "catholic"?

The term "catholic" means "according to the whole." The Church is called "catholic" because it holds the whole faith once and for all delivered to the saints and maintains unity with the Church of the Apostles throughout time and space. (#95)

Biblical History

Tell me about the Ten Commandments and Desert Wandering.

After escaping Egypt, the Lord taught Moses the Law and how to worship God and led the people to the promised land, but the people of Israel disobeyed God again and again. When the Israelites failed to trust God's promise for the tenth time, they were made to wander the desert for 40 years so that only their children, led by Joshua, would inherit the land promised by God.

WEEK 12

Apostles' Creed

I believe in God, the Father almighty, creator of heaven and earth.	Father
I believe in Jesus Christ, his only Son, our Lord. He was conceived by the Holy Spirit and born of the Virgin Mary. He suffered under Pontius Pilate, was crucified, died, and was buried. He descended to the dead. On the third day, he rose again. He ascended into heaven, and is seated at the right hand of the Father. He will come again to judge the living and the dead.	Son
I believe in the Holy Spirit, the holy catholic Church, the communion of saints, the forgiveness of sins, the resurrection of the body, and the life everlasting. Amen.	Holy Spirit

Catechesis

What is the "communion of saints?"

The communion of the saints is the unity and fellowship of all those united in one Body and one Spirit in Holy Baptism, both those on earth and those in heaven. (#99) (Ephesians 4:4–5; Hebrews 12:1)

Biblical History

Tell me about Joshua and the Conquest of the Land.

After Moses and his generation had died, Joshua became the leader of the Israelites. After 40 years in the wilderness, the people of Israel crossed the Jordan River and held the first Passover in the Promised Land. As God commanded, Joshua then led the Israelites in their conquest against the Canaanites, beginning in the city of Jericho. (Joshua 1–6)

God's Word

(Weeks 13–17)

WEEK 13

Bible Verse

All Scripture is breathed out by God and profitable

for teaching, for reproof, for correction, and for training in righteousness,

that the man of God may be complete, equipped for every good work.

2 Tim 3:16–17

Catechesis

How does God forgive your sins?

By virtue of Christ's atoning sacrifice, God sets aside my sins, accepts me, and adopts me as his child and heir in Jesus Christ. Loving me as his child, he forgives my sins whenever I turn to him in repentance and faith. (#135) (2 Corinthians 5:16–18)

Biblical History

Tell me about the Battle of Jericho.

Jericho was a city in the Promised Land with a huge wall around it. The Israelites, obeying God, crossed the Jordan River carrying the Ark of the Covenant and marched around Jericho for seven days. On the seventh day, the Israelites marched around Jericho seven times, then Joshua told the people to shout for the Lord, and the city walls came crashing down. (Joshua 6)

NOTES:

WEEK 14

Bible Verse

All Scripture is breathed out by God and profitable

for teaching, for reproof, for correction, and for training in righteousness,

that the man of God may be complete, equipped for every good work.

2 Tim 3:16–17

Catechesis

How should you learn the Bible?

I should seek to know the whole of Scripture and to memorize key passages for my own spiritual growth and for sharing with others. (#228)

Biblical History

Tell me about Judges.

After Joshua the Lord appointed Judges to protect his people and turn their eyes back to Him; there were 12 judges in all. These Judges were civil and military leaders that commanded the people of Israel against the Canaanites and warned the people against worshiping false gods. Deborah, the only female judge, was a prophet and military leader appointed by God. She led the armies of Israel against attacks from the Canaanites. (Judges 4:1–12)

NOTES:

WEEK 15

Bible Verse

Trust in the Lord with all your heart,

and do not lean on your own understanding.

In all your ways acknowledge him,

and he will make straight your paths.

Proverbs 3:5–6

Catechesis

How should you pray?

I should pray with humility, love, and a ready openness to God's will, in my heart hearing God say, "be still and know that I am God." (#237) (Psalm 46:10–11; 2 Chronicles 7:14–15; Philippians 4:6)

Biblical History

Tell me about the Former Prophets.

In the Jewish tradition, "Former Prophets" are the historical and prophetic Books of Joshua, Judges, first and second Samuel, and first and second Kings. The main theme of the Former Prophets is obedience to the Lord. The Former Prophets cover the story of Israel in the Promised Land: gaining the land, living in the land, abusing the land, and losing the land.

NOTES:

WEEK 16

Bible Verse

Trust in the Lord with all your heart,

and do not lean on your own understanding.

In all your ways acknowledge him,

and he will make straight your paths.

Proverbs 3:5–6

Catechesis

What is grace?

Grace is the gift of God's love, mercy, and help, which he freely gives to us who, because of our sin, deserve only condemnation. (#137) (Acts 20:32; Romans 3:24; 2 Corinthians 8:9; Ephesians 1:6–7)

Biblical History

Tell me about the Kingship of Israel.

The Kingdom of Israel was united during the reigns of three kings, Saul, David, and Solomon. Each king reigned for forty years. Saul battled the Philistines and later disobeyed God. David was the Lord's chosen one, a musician and warrior, but he also disobeyed God. Solomon, son of David, was the final king and built the first Temple in Jerusalem. King Solomon also ended up disobeying God. After this, the kingdom of Israel split in two, Israel and Juda, after King Solomon's son, Rehoboam, became king. (1 Samuel 9; 2 Samuel 5; 1 Kings 2)

NOTES:

WEEK 17

Bible Verse

Trust in the Lord with all your heart,

and do not lean on your own understanding.

In all your ways acknowledge him,

and he will make straight your paths.

Proverbs 3:5–6

Catechesis

How does the New Testament teach you to view the church?

Holy Scripture teaches me to view the Church as God's family, as the body and bride of Christ, and as the temple where God in Christ dwells by his Spirit. (#90) (John 1:12; 1 Peter 2:9–10, 1 Corinthians 3:16–17; 2 Corinthians 6:16–7:1; Revelation 19:6–10; 21:9–10)

Biblical History

Tell me about David and Goliath.

David, who was not king yet, was on his way to play music for Saul. He heard about the threat of the Philistine giant, Goliath, and the prize if defeated. David set out to battle Goliath with five stones saying, "I have come against you in the name of the Lord Almighty." David's faith in God helped in defeating Goliath. (1 Samuel 17)

NOTES:

The Lord's Prayer

(Weeks 18–26)

WEEK 18

The Lord's Prayer

Good Children, it is important to know that you are not able to do these things on your own, nor to follow his commandments, nor to serve him without special grace, which you must learn at all times to call for by diligent prayer. Let me hear if you can say the Lord's Prayer:

Our Father, Who art in heaven,
hallowed be thy name.
Thy Kingdom come,
Thy will be done on earth, as it is in heaven:
Give us this day our daily bread
and forgive us our trespasses, as we forgive those who trespass against us.
And lead us not into temptation
but deliver us from evil.

For thine is the kingdom, and the power,
and the glory, for ever and ever. Amen.

Catechesis

Why should you pray the Lord's Prayer?

I should pray the Lord's Prayer because Christ in the gospels teaches it to his disciples, as both a practice and a pattern for fellowship with God the Father. (#157) (Matthew 6:9–13; Luke 11:2–4).

Biblical History

Tell me about Elijah on Mount Carmel.

The people of Israel turned away from God again, and he punished them by not sending rain for three years. But God never turned his back on them and sent his prophet Elijah to Mount Carmel to remind the people of Israel of God's love for them. Elijah built an altar in the name of the Lord, poured water over the wood and the offering, and then the fire of the Lord consumed it. When the people saw this, they repented and returned to God, and the Lord sent them rain. (1 Kings 18)

WEEK 19

The Lord's Prayer

Good Children, it is important to know that you are not able to do these things on your own, nor to follow his commandments, nor to serve him without special grace, which you must learn at all times to call for by diligent prayer. Let me hear if you can say the Lord's Prayer:

Our Father, Who art in heaven,
hallowed be thy name.
Thy Kingdom come,
Thy will be done on earth, as it is in heaven:
Give us this day our daily bread
and forgive us our trespasses, as we forgive those who trespass against us.
And lead us not into temptation
but deliver us from evil.

For thine is the kingdom, and the power,
and the glory, for ever and ever. Amen.

Catechesis

If your Father is in heaven, can he help you on earth?

Yes. God is everywhere, and as my almighty Father in heaven, he is able and willing to answer my prayers. (#168) (Psalm 99; Isaiah 6; Ephesians 3:20; 4:6)

Biblical History

Tell me about Israel's Divided Kingdom.

The nation rebelled due to high taxes and Israel divided into two kingdoms. The southern kingdom was made up of the tribes of Judah and Benjamin, becoming the kingdom of Judah. The ten remaining northern tribes became known as Israel. Except for some good kings in Judah, like Hezekiah and Josiah, the rulers of both kingdoms engaged in wickedness and idolatry. (1 Kings 12–25; 2 Kings; 2 Chronicles 10–36; Obadiah and Joel)

WEEK 20

The Lord's Prayer

Good Children, it is important to know that you are not able to do these things on your own, nor to follow his commandments, nor to serve him without special grace, which you must learn at all times to call for by diligent prayer. Let me hear if you can say the Lord's Prayer:

Our Father, Who art in heaven,
hallowed be thy name.
Thy Kingdom come,
Thy will be done on earth, as it is in heaven:
Give us this day our daily bread
and forgive us our trespasses, as we forgive those who trespass against us.
And lead us not into temptation
but deliver us from evil.

For thine is the kingdom, and the power,
and the glory, for ever and ever. Amen.

Catechesis

What does "hallowed" mean?

Hallowed means to be treated as holy, set apart, and sacred. To hallow God's name is to honor him as holy. (#172)

Biblical History

Tell me about the Latter Prophets.

The Latter Prophets are the historical and prophetic books of the major prophets Isaiah, Jeremiah, Ezekiel, and the twelve minor Prophets. They spoke as messengers of God. After the kingdom split, the prophets were sent to warn the people of Israel, the northern kingdom, of their disobedience to God and worship of false idols.

WEEK 21

The Lord's Prayer

Good Children, it is important to know that you are not able to do these things on your own, nor to follow his commandments, nor to serve him without special grace, which you must learn at all times to call for by diligent prayer. Let me hear if you can say the Lord's Prayer:

Our Father, Who art in heaven,
hallowed be thy name.
Thy Kingdom come,
Thy will be done on earth, as it is in heaven:
Give us this day our daily bread
and forgive us our trespasses, as we forgive those who trespass against us.
And lead us not into temptation
but deliver us from evil.

For thine is the kingdom, and the power,
and the glory, for ever and ever. Amen.

Catechesis

How do you live in God's Kingdom?

My Kingdom life as a Christian consists of living with joy, hope, and peace as a child of God, a citizen of heaven, and a faithful follower of Jesus Christ. (#180) (Romans 14:17; Ephesians 4–6; Colossians 1: 13–14; 3:4; 1 Thessalonians 4:11)

Biblical History

Tell me about the Northern Kingdom falling to Assyria.

After Israel ignored the prophet's warnings, the Northern Kingdom fell to the attack of the Assyrian Empire. Isaiah had warned Israel if they did not repent, God would use the Assyrian Empire to destroy them. The ten tribes were taken into captivity, and the people of the northern kingdom were scattered, and their Hebrew identity was lost. (Isaiah 6; 2 Kings 17:6–41)

WEEK 22

The Lord's Prayer

Good Children, it is important to know that you are not able to do these things on your own, nor to follow his commandments, nor to serve him without special grace, which you must learn at all times to call for by diligent prayer. Let me hear if you can say the Lord's Prayer:

Our Father, Who art in heaven,
hallowed be thy name.
Thy Kingdom come,
Thy will be done on earth, as it is in heaven:
Give us this day our daily bread
and forgive us our trespasses, as we forgive those who trespass against us.
And lead us not into temptation
but deliver us from evil.

For thine is the kingdom, and the power,
and the glory, for ever and ever. Amen.

Catechesis

Where can you find God's will?

I find the will of God outlined in the Ten Commandments, learn its fullness from the whole of Scripture, and see it end up in the Law of Christ, which calls for my complete love of God and my neighbor. (#183) (Deuteronomy 29:29; Psalms 119:1–16, 104–105, Proverbs 4; John 13:34; Acts 7:51–53; Galatians 6:2)

Biblical History

Tell me about Judah falling to Babylon, the First Temple destroyed.

The Assyrian Empire also tried to attack the Kingdom of Judah. King Hezekiah prepared his people but also prayed to God to deliver them from war. God struck down the Assyrians outside of Jerusalem, and Judah survived the assault. Years later, Jerusalem fell to Babylon's King Nebuchadnezzar II. He destroyed King Solomon's Temple, and the people of Judah became captives of Babylon for 70 years. (Daniel 1)

WEEK 23

The Lord's Prayer

Good Children, it is important to know that you are not able to do these things on your own, nor to follow his commandments, nor to serve him without special grace, which you must learn at all times to call for by diligent prayer. Let me hear if you can say the Lord's Prayer:

Our Father, Who art in heaven,
hallowed be thy name.
Thy Kingdom come,
Thy will be done on earth, as it is in heaven:
Give us this day our daily bread
and forgive us our trespasses, as we forgive those who trespass against us.
And lead us not into temptation
but deliver us from evil.

For thine is the kingdom, and the power,
and the glory, for ever and ever. Amen.

Catechesis

What does "our daily bread" mean?

Daily bread includes all that is needed for me to grow up happy and healthy, like food and clothing, homes and families, work and health, friends and neighbors, and peace in our country. (#188) (Matthew 6:8; Luke 11:12; 1 Timothy 2:1–2)

Biblical History

Tell me about Esther and the King.

After the Persian King Artaxerxes banished his first wife, he married a Jewish girl named Esther, but he did not know she was Jewish. When one of Artaxerxes' advisors convinced the King to kill all of the Israelites in his kingdom, Esther revealed to the king that she was also from Israel. Esther stays faithful to God even in a culture that does not acknowledge Him and she saved all of her people through her courage.

WEEK 24

The Lord's Prayer

Good Children, it is important to know that you are not able to do these things on your own, nor to follow his commandments, nor to serve him without special grace, which you must learn at all times to call for by diligent prayer. Let me hear if you can say the Lord's Prayer:

Our Father, Who art in heaven,
hallowed be thy name.
Thy Kingdom come,
Thy will be done on earth, as it is in heaven:
Give us this day our daily bread
and forgive us our trespasses, as we forgive those who trespass against us.
And lead us not into temptation
but deliver us from evil.

For thine is the kingdom, and the power,
and the glory, for ever and ever. Amen.

Catechesis

Does God forgive your sins?

Yes! God freely forgives the sins of all who ask him in true repentance and faith, and that includes me. (#196) (Leviticus 6:6–8; Matthew 11:28–30; John 6:37, 40, 51; 7:37; 2 Corinthians 5:17–21; Hebrews 7:25)

Biblical History

Tell me about Daniel, Nebuchadnezzar, and the Lion's Den.

Daniel, the prophet, was favored by the kings of Babylon, but other officials were jealous of him. The officials convinced King Darius to make a law that no one was to pray to any man or god except to the king for thirty days. Daniel prayed to God, even though it was against the law, and when the king found out, he was forced to throw Daniel into a lion's den. The next day, everyone was amazed to see that Daniel had not been harmed by the lions. An angel of the Lord had protected Daniel. (Daniel 6)

WEEK 25

The Lord's Prayer

Good Children, it is important to know that you are not able to do these things on your own, nor to follow his commandments, nor to serve him without special grace, which you must learn at all times to call for by diligent prayer. Let me hear if you can say the Lord's Prayer:

Our Father, Who art in heaven,
hallowed be thy name.
Thy Kingdom come,
Thy will be done on earth, as it is in heaven:
Give us this day our daily bread
and forgive us our trespasses, as we forgive those who trespass against us.
And lead us not into temptation
but deliver us from evil.

For thine is the kingdom, and the power,
and the glory, for ever and ever. Amen.

Catechesis

What is temptation?

Temptation is something that lures us to abandon total trust in God or to violate his commandments. (#202) (Proverbs 1:8–19; James 1:14–15)

Biblical History

Tell me about the Fall of Babylon.

After the Babylonian Empire destroyed Jerusalem and the tribe of Judah had lived in exile for 70 years, Babylon fell to the Persians. The Jewish prophets Isaiah, Jeremiah, and Daniel prophesied that this would happen. The Persian king, Cyrus the Great, captured Babylon and released the Jewish people from their captivity, promising to rebuild the Temple in Jerusalem, which he did. (Isaiah 47; Jeremiah 51; Daniel 2; Ezra 1–6)

WEEK 26

The Lord's Prayer

Good Children, it is important to know that you are not able to do these things on your own, nor to follow his commandments, nor to serve him without special grace, which you must learn at all times to call for by diligent prayer. Let me hear if you can say the Lord's Prayer:

Our Father, Who art in heaven,
hallowed be thy name.
Thy Kingdom come,
Thy will be done on earth, as it is in heaven:
Give us this day our daily bread
and forgive us our trespasses, as we forgive those who trespass against us.
And lead us not into temptation
but deliver us from evil.

For thine is the kingdom, and the power,
and the glory, for ever and ever. Amen.

Catechesis

If God made the world good at its creation, why does he permit evil?

God made us free to worship, love, and obey him, but also free to reject his love, rebel against him and choose evil—as the human race has done. (#209) (Genesis 6:5; Ecclesiastes 7:29; 1 Timothy 1:20; Revelation 2:18–29)

Biblical History

Tell me about the Jews returning and rebuilding the Temple.

When the Persians captured Babylon, "the Lord stirred up the spirit of King Cyrus" (Ezra 1:1). The Persian king allowed the exiled Jews to return to Jerusalem, the capital of Judah, to rebuild their temple. The rebuilding of the Temple took so long that there were three other kings of Persia after Cyrus before it was finished during the reign of King Darius II. (Ezra 1–6)

The Ten Commandments

(Weeks 27–29)

WEEK 27

Ten Commandments (Exodus 20:7–17; Deuteronomy 5:11–21)

You said your parents and church promised that you should keep God's Commandments.
What are they?

Thou shalt...
1. have no other gods before me.
2. not make unto thee any graven image.
3. not take the name of the LORD thy God in vain
4. remember the sabbath day, to keep it holy.
5. honor thy father and thy mother: that thy days may be long upon the land which the LORD thy God giveth thee.
6. not murder.
7. not commit adultery.
8. not steal.
9. not bear false witness against thy neighbor.
10. not covet.

Catechesis

What do you chiefly learn by these commandments?

I learn two things: my duty toward God and my duty toward my neighbor.

Biblical History

Tell me about the return from Babylon.

Nehemiah, one of the Latter Prophets, fasted and prayed to God to return to his home in Jerusalem. His request from the Persian king, Artaxerxes, was to return to Jerusalem to rebuild the city. After inspecting the broken gates and walls of Jerusalem, Nehemiah led the Israelites to rise up and rebuild the city. Nehemiah and Ezra help repopulate Jerusalem and re-establish the laws of Moses which they found in the ruins of the temple. (Nehemiah 2–8; 2 Kings 22)

WEEK 28

Ten Commandments (Exodus 20:7–17; Deuteronomy 5:11–21)

You said your parents and church promised that you should keep God's Commandments. What are they?

Thou shalt…
1. have no other gods before me.
2. not make unto thee any graven image.
3. not take the name of the LORD thy God in vain
4. remember the sabbath day, to keep it holy.
5. honor thy father and thy mother: that thy days may be long upon the land which the LORD thy God giveth thee.
6. not murder.
7. not commit adultery.
8. not steal.
9. not bear false witness against thy neighbor.
10. not covet.

Catechesis

What is your duty towards God?

My duty towards God is to believe in him, to fear him, and to love him with all my heart, my mind, my soul, my strength; to worship him, to give him thanks, to put my whole trust in him, to call upon him, to honor his holy Name and Word, and to serve him truly all the days of my life.

Biblical History

Tell me about the close of the Old Testament Prophets.

The Old Testament ends with Malachi, "messenger of God," and the last of the twelve minor prophets. Malachi's message came after the Temple and land were restored, but soon the Israelites began to disobey God again! Malachi told the people that if they continued neglecting God, their sacrifices and prayers would go unanswered, and God would turn away from them again. Only those people who remember God will be remembered by God. (Malachi 1–3)

WEEK 29

Ten Commandments (Exodus 20:7–17; Deuteronomy 5:11–21)

You said your parents and church promised that you should keep God's Commandments. What are they?

Thou shalt…
1. have no other gods before me.
2. not make unto thee any graven image.
3. not take the name of the LORD thy God in vain
4. remember the sabbath day, to keep it holy.
5. honor thy father and thy mother: that thy days may be long upon the land which the LORD thy God giveth thee.
6. not murder.
7. not commit adultery.
8. not steal.
9. not bear false witness against thy neighbor.
10. not covet.

Catechesis

What is your duty towards your neighbor?

My duty towards my neighbor is to love him as myself and to do to all people as I would have done to me. To love, honor, and listen to my parents; to honor and obey the law, my teachers, and my bishops and priests; to act humbly to my neighbor; to hurt nobody by word or deed; to be just and true in everything I do; to never hate anyone in my heart; to keep my hands from picking and stealing and my tongue from gossiping, lying, and slandering; to keep my body in temperance, thoughtfulness, and chastity; not to covet or desire other people's belongings; but to learn and work hard to make my own living and to follow God's call in my life.

Biblical History

Tell me about the Desecration of the Temple by Antiochus IV.

In 167 BC, King Antiochus IV of Syria, took control of Jerusalem. The king offered the sacrifice of a pig on the temple's altar to worship Zeus. By doing this, the Temple was desecrated. This action was an attack on the Jewish people, their religious rites, and traditions.

The Sacraments

(Weeks 30–40)

WEEK 30

Bible Verse

For by grace, you have been saved through faith. And this is not your own doing; it is the gift of God, not a result of works, so that no one may boast. For we are his workmanship, created in Christ Jesus for good works, which God prepared beforehand, that we should walk in them.

Ephesians 2:8–10

Catechesis

What is a sacrament?

A sacrament is an outward and visible sign of an inward and spiritual grace. God gives us the sign as a means through which we receive that grace, and as a real promise that we do in fact receive it. (#102) (1662 Catechism)

Biblical History

Tell me about the Maccabean Revolt.

From 167–160 BC, during the Hellenistic period, Jewish rebels waged a war against the control of King Antiochus IV after the king banned Jewish practices and desecrated the temple in Jerusalem. The Maccabees, led by Judah Maccabee, fought for independence from the Greek Empire and destroyed Greek religious altars. Eventually, the King removed the ban on Jewish practices, but the Maccabees kept fighting for many years afterward.

NOTES:

WEEK 31

Bible Verse

For by grace, you have been saved through faith. And this is not your own doing; it is the gift of God, not a result of works, so that no one may boast. For we are his workmanship, created in Christ Jesus for good works, which God prepared beforehand, that we should walk in them.

Ephesians 2:8–10

Catechesis

How should you receive the sacraments?

I should receive the sacraments by faith in Christ, with repentance and thanksgiving. I need Faith in Christ to receive grace, and I need obedience to Christ for the benefits of the sacraments to bear fruit in my life. (#103) (1662 Catechisms; Articles of Religion, 28)

Biblical History

Tell me about Hanukkah.

During the Maccabean Revolt in 164 BC, the rebels recaptured the city of Jerusalem, and cleansed and rededicated the Temple. Hanukkah, known as the "Festival of Lights," is an eight-day Jewish holiday that celebrates this rededication of the temple to the worship of God.

NOTES:

WEEK 32

Bible Verse

For by grace, you have been saved through faith. And this is not your own doing; it is the gift of God, not a result of works, so that no one may boast. For we are his workmanship, created in Christ Jesus for good works, which God prepared beforehand, that we should walk in them.

Ephesians 2:8–10

Catechesis

What are the sacraments of the Gospel?

The two sacraments ordained by Christ, which are generally necessary for our salvation, are **Baptism and Holy Communion**, which is also known as the Lord's Supper or the Holy Eucharist. (#104) (Articles of Religion, 25)

Biblical History

Tell me about the Hasmonean Dynasty.

The Hasmonean Dynasty ruled over Judaea after the Maccabean Revolt until the Roman Republic conquered Israel in 37 BC. During the re-organizing and renewal of the Hebrew nation under the Hasmonean Dynasty, the two dominant sects of the Jewish faith were the Sadducees and the Pharisees.

NOTES:

WEEK 33

Bible Verse

And Peter said to them, "Repent and be baptized every one of you

in the name of Jesus Christ for the forgiveness of your sins,

and you will receive the gift of the Holy Spirit.

Acts 2:38

Catechesis

What is the outward and visible sign in Baptism?

The outward and visible sign is water, in which we are baptized "in the name of the Father, and of the Son, and of the Holy Spirit"—the name of the Triune God to whom we are being committed. (#105) (1662 Catechism, 1 Peter 3:21; Matthew 28:19)

Biblical History

Tell me about the Roman General Pompey.

In 63 BC, Pompey was asked to help solve a conflict between two brothers who were fighting over the Jewish throne. When Pompey arrived in Judaea, one brother surrendered but his supporters refused to give up Jerusalem. After laying siege for three months, the Romans finally controlled all of Jerusalem. This was the end of the Hasmonean Dynasty and Judaea was broken apart and became a part of the Roman Republic.

NOTES:

WEEK 34

Bible Verse

And Peter said to them, "Repent and be baptized every one of you

in the name of Jesus Christ for the forgiveness of your sins,

and you will receive the gift of the Holy Spirit.

Acts 2:38

Catechesis

What is required of you when you come to be baptized?

Repentance, in which I turn away from sin; and faith, in which I turn to Jesus Christ as my Savior and Lord and embrace the promises that God makes to me in this sacrament. (#107) (Acts 2:38)

Biblical History

Tell me about the birth of John and Jesus.

During the reign of King Herod, God sent an angel to visit the priest Zechariah to tell him he and his wife Elizabeth would bear a son who would become John the Baptist. God also sent the angel Gabriel to Joseph and his fiancé, Mary. He told her that she would bear a son through the Holy Spirit, and his name would be Jesus, and he would be the Son of God. (Luke 1:5–38)

NOTES:

WEEK 35

Bible Verse

And Peter said to them, "Repent and be baptized every one of you in the name of Jesus Christ for the forgiveness of your sins, and you will receive the gift of the Holy Spirit.

Acts 2:38

Catechesis

What signs of the Holy Spirit's work do you hope and pray to see as a result of your baptism?

I hope and pray that the Holy Spirit who dwells within me will help me to be an active member of my Christian community, participate in worship, continually repent and return to God, proclaim the faith, love and serve my neighbor, and strive for justice and peace. (#109) (Hebrews 10:16–17)

Biblical History

Tell me about Jesus going to the Temple.

"Now his parents went to Jerusalem every year at the Feast of the Passover. And when he was twelve years old, they went up according to custom. And when the feast was ended, as they were returning, the boy Jesus stayed behind in Jerusalem. After three days they found him in the temple, sitting among the teachers, listening to them and asking them questions. And all who heard him were amazed at his understanding and his answers." (Luke 2:41–43, 46–47)

NOTES:

WEEK 36

Bible Verse

And he took bread, and when he had given thanks, he broke it and gave it to them, saying, "This is my body, which is given for you. Do this in remembrance of me."

Luke 22:19

Catechesis

Why did Christ institute the sacrament of Holy Communion?

He instituted it for the continued remembrance of the sacrifice of his atoning death, and to carry the benefits the faithful receive through that sacrifice. (#110) (Luke 22:17–20; 1 Corinthians 10:16–17)

Biblical History

Tell me about the ministry of Jesus in the Four Gospels.

Around AD 27–29, the ministry of Jesus began with his baptism at the Jordan River by his cousin, John the Baptist. Jesus traveled throughout Israel teaching and preaching, casting out demons, and healing the sick. The four Gospels—Matthew, Mark, Luke and John—tell different perspectives of Jesus' life and ministry. The word gospel means "good news."

NOTES:

WEEK 37

Bible Verse

And he took bread, and when he had given thanks, he broke it

and gave it to them, saying, "This is my body, which is given for you.

Do this in remembrance of me."

Luke 22:19

Catechesis

What is the outward and visible sign in Holy Communion?

The visible sign is bread and wine, which Christ commands us to receive. (#111)
(1 Corinthians 11:23)

Biblical History

Tell me about the Sermon on the Mount.

The Sermon on the Mount is the most famous sermon that Jesus gave. He sat on a mountainside in front of crowds of people and his disciples and taught them about love and humility. These teachings are called the Beatitudes. Jesus taught the central ideas of what it means to be a follower of Christ.

NOTES:

WEEK 38

Bible Verse

And he took bread, and when he had given thanks, he broke it

and gave it to them, saying, "This is my body, which is given for you.

Do this in remembrance of me."

Luke 22:19

Catechesis

What is required of you when you come to receive Holy Communion?

I am to think about myself. Do I truly repent of my sins and intend to lead a new life in Christ? Do I have a living faith in God's mercy through Christ and am I thankful for his atoning death that saved me? And have I shown love and forgiveness to my family and to all the people I know and have met? (#114) (1 Corinthians 11:27–32)

Biblical History

Tell me about Jesus' arrest and crucifixion.

After the Last Supper Jesus and his disciples went to the garden of Gethsemane. Jesus went to pray to God about the burden of saving mankind. An angel appeared to Jesus and strengthened him. Jesus was arrested, condemned, and handed over to Pontius Pilate, the Roman Governor of Jerusalem, the next day. Jesus was beaten and hung on a cross by the Romans next to two thieves. Jesus loves me so much that he died on the cross to save me.

NOTES:

WEEK 39

Bible Verse

Rejoice in the Lord always; again, I will say, rejoice.

Let your reasonableness be known to everyone.

The Lord is at hand; do not be anxious about anything,

but in everything by prayer and supplication with thanksgiving

let your requests be made known to God.

And the peace of God, which surpasses all understanding,

will guard your hearts and your minds in Christ Jesus.

Philippians 4:4–6

Catechesis

Are there other sacraments?

Other sacraments include confirmation, absolution, ordination, marriage, and anointing of the sick. These are sometimes called the sacraments of the Church. (#116)

Biblical History

Tell me about the Resurrection and Ascension of Jesus.

Jesus came back from the dead on the third day, and he went to visit his disciples. After he blessed them and told them to wait for the Holy Spirit, God lifted Jesus into the heavens where Jesus sits at the right hand of God. Ascension Day is a major feast day in the Christian calendar! (Luke 24, Acts 1:6–11)

NOTES:

WEEK 40

Bible Verse

Rejoice in the Lord always; again, I will say, rejoice.

Let your reasonableness be known to everyone.

The Lord is at hand; do not be anxious about anything,

but in everything by prayer and supplication with thanksgiving

let your requests be made known to God.

And the peace of God, which surpasses all understanding,

will guard your hearts and your minds in Christ Jesus.

Philippians 4:4–6

Catechesis

Of what should you be certain in prayer?

I should be certain that God hears my prayers. I should also be certain that in response, he will grant me all that I actually need, by his wisdom, in his time, and for his glory. (#238) (Deuteronomy 6:24; Esther 4:16; Proverbs 15:29; Ephesians 3:14–21)

Biblical History

Tell me about Pentecost.

Pentecost came after Jesus ascended to Heaven. A rush of wind came, and tongues of fire rested on each disciple. The Holy Spirit began to speak through them. People from every nation heard them speaking in their own language. The disciples told the crowds about Jesus, converting them to the Christian faith, and forming the early church. (Acts 2)

NOTES:

Glossary of Terms

Ascend—to move or go upward
Absolution—release from consequences; a freeing from blame or guilt
Atonement—the reconciliation of God and humankind
Creed—a statement of belief
Disciple—a personal follower or student of Jesus
Patriarch—the male head of a family or tribe
Prophetic—accurately describing or predicting what will happen in the future
Repent—to feel or express sincere regret about one's wrongdoing
Resurrect—restore to life
Sacrament—a religious ceremony regarded as imparting divine grace such as baptism and the Eucharist
Supplication—the action of asking or begging for something humbly
Temptation—the desire to do something, especially something wrong or unwise
Virtue—behavior showing high moral standards

Memory Work Sample Ideas for the First Six Weeks

Week	Bible Verse or Creed	Catechesis	Biblical History
1	Read aloud 2 times.** While reciting, do jumping jacks, do the twist, balance on 1 leg.	Read aloud 2 times. Learn some hand motions. Recite several times using the hand motions.	Read aloud 2 times. Erase a few words and read, continue until some or all words are erased.
2	Read before the feather falls to the ground. Drop a feather from high up! This is good for shorter memory work.	Read aloud 2 times. Play Stand and Sit: First student/parent says as much of the sentence as he/she wants, when he/she pauses the next student picks up where they left off. Do this faster each time you repeat!	Read aloud 2 times. Take some words from the sentences and make them out of clay or playdoh. When you tell the story again, have the kids show what they made when they hear that word.
3	Read aloud 2 times. Do squats, jump rope, do the floss dance, arm circles.	Read aloud 2 times. Make up hand motions together.	Read aloud 2 times. Write the history sentence on a white board. Erase a word or phrase every time you recite. Try to repeat this 4 times. If you don't have an erase board, print out words/phrases/sentences, lay it out in order then start taking some out as you recite and repeat.
4	Read aloud 2 times. Use a silly voice each time you recite.	Read aloud 2 times. Toss a ball or stuffed animal around while reciting. Pick up the pace each time you repeat.	Read aloud 2 times. Assign some motions to a few of the words in the sentences. When you recite, do those motions for those words.
5	Read aloud 2 times. Trade places with your child and have them be the teacher.	Read aloud 2 times. Mimic an animal each time you recite. For example, say it while being an elephant, frog, gorilla, etc.	Read aloud 2 times. Sentence scramble: Print out the history sentences and cut them into single words or phrases. Scramble them up and have the kids put it in order. They can race against you!
6	Read aloud 2 times. Assume a superhero pose, crunches, bicycle legs in the air, crab walk, laying on the floor, upside down, etc. Have fun!	Read aloud 2 times. Play Popcorn. Circle a few words and jump up, clap, snap etc. every time that word is said during recitation.	Read aloud 2 times. Print out the sentences in sections to do hopscotch with.

For these and other ideas, see this YouTube channel: Karina Taylor @karinataylor3092

**Reading aloud two times is important because you are receiving the information for the very first time. It also helps to make sure pronunciation of words is correct. Make notes in your curriculum book on what worked best for your child.